Pray in 30 Days the Affirmative Way

By Lori H. Huggins

Pray in 30 Days
the Affirmative Way

Copyright ©2021 by Lori H. Huggins

Printed in the United States of America
ISBN #978-1-7357752-6-5

All rights are reserved solely by the author.
The author declares that the contents are original and
do not infringe on the rights of any other person.

No part of this book may be reproduced in any form except with
permission from the author. The views in this book are
not necessarily the views of the publisher.

Table of Contents

Introduction .... Page VI

DAY 1: Lessons Lead To Victory .... Page 8

DAY 2: Creativity And Completion .... Page 9

DAY 3: Growth In Darkness .... Page 10

DAY 4: Strength In Surrender .... Page 11

DAY 5: Preserved For Purpose .... Page 12

DAY 6: Valuable Relationships .... Page 13

DAY 7: Revive Us Again .... Page 14

DAY 8: The Pain, The Push, The Power .... Page 15

DAY 9: Health Is Wealth .... Page 16

DAY 10: Serenity In The Suffering .... Page 17

DAY 11: Expanded Awareness .... Page 18

DAY 12: The Law Of Reciprocity .... Page 19

DAY 13: Heal The World .... Page 20

DAY 14: A Brand New Day .... Page 21

DAY 15: One With God And One With All .... Page 22

Table of Contents

DAY 16: Living, Moving, In My Being .... Page 23

DAY 17: Nothing Missing, Nothing Broken .... Page 24

DAY 18: Blessed To Be A Blessing .... Page 25

DAY 19: Yes And Amen .... Page 26

DAY 20: Prayer For Immunity .... Page 27

DAY 21: We Surrender .... Page 28

DAY 22: Gratitude .... Page 29

DAY 23: I Am Free .... Page 30

DAY 24: It Is Working For My Good .... Page 31

DAY 25: One Power And One Presence .... Page 32

DAY 26: I Speak .... Page 33

DAY 27: Behold The Glory .... Page 34

DAY 28: It's All In Me .... Page 35

DAY 29: Take Nothing For Granted .... Page 36

DAY 30: Just For You .... Page 37

Conclusion .... Page 38

For You, The Reader

This book was birthed in Spring 2020 when the global pandemic began to sweep through the planet. I began to listen to people in traditional churches pray regarding the abrupt loss of life that was ravishing the nation and the globe, and I did not like what I was hearing; my Spirit was grieved. It felt as if spiritual leaders were not praying with their God-given authority and that the prayers of many sounded aimless, lacking the force needed to deal with the global crisis at hand. I began to listen to ministers in the Christian New Thought movement who utilized a method called Affirmative Prayer, which I had studied in the days of my youth from books in my mother's home library. I noticed that they prayed differently, with an authority that elevated my faith level into believing that the declarative, creative tone of our prayers have the power to radically transform situations in both the supernatural realm and the natural realm for the highest good of humanity.

Introduction

Affirmative prayer is an effective prayer method used in contrast to pleading and begging God to intervene on our behalf; this prayer strategy enables us to verbalize positive assertions that focus on the prayer outcome rather than the problem. Jesus the Christ laid the foundation and gave us the blueprint for affirmative prayer when he said, "I tell you, you can pray for anything, and if you believe that you've received it, it will be yours." (Mark 11:24).

30 Days of Affirmative Prayer

DAY 1:
Lessons Lead To Victory

All-powerful, omniscient, creative force of the universe, I come before you with thanksgiving, joy, and gratitude for this day. I give thanks for the sun, the rain, and for all lessons that have come my way in this life. I thank you for the ability to learn from the lessons, to overcome challenges in the face of adversity, and to rise above obstacles that may be ahead of me. I use adversity to find untapped strength, and with the help of the Holy Spirit, I turn pain into power. I walk victoriously. I walk with an expectancy of things that only work to support my highest good. The universe and everything good in it is working for my best interest. If God is good, then I AM good.

Today's Focus: *Everything is manifesting for my highest good.*

DAY 2:

Creativity And Completion

Creative Holy Spirit, I thank you for the creativity that you have placed in me, for shaping my heart after the image and likeness of your divine nature. Each day I grow in faith, integrity, character, love, and service. My heart is devoted to You due to your loving kindness and who You are. Holy Spirit, you are great, and you are doing the miraculous by way of healing mentally, emotionally, and physically. Wholeness is mine, and joy is mine as I walk in the freedom of your divine grace while living out Your balanced and perfect law.

Today's Focus: *I am an open vessel for which divine creative energy flows.*

DAY 3:
Growth In Darkness

Dear Holy Spirit, it is with a thankful heart that I thank you for both the light and the darkness, for it is in the darkness that seeds are planted, and then they are forced to grow up and out, toward the light. The light helps to pull us out of the darkness and then guide us into all truth. As we enter into the light and remain there, we are steadfast, and unwavering. Continue, sweet Spirit, to help us become more energized and enthusiastic about your will for our lives. Day by day, we pray for divine character and an encounter with the Creator that radically transforms us into the divine beings God has designed us to be.

Today's Focus: *I choose to let the radiant light of God in me shine in the darkness.*

DAY 4:
Strength In Surrender

Most High God, Creator of the heavens and the earth! You are magnificent, beneficent, and merciful. I thank you for the strength to live each day and face the days ahead with the internal fortitude that only comes from Your divine power. I surrender my being to you, Holy Spirit, knowing that by putting all of my trust in you, I am divinely kept and prepared for the great and mighty things you have in store for my life and all who are attached to me. In your name, I pray, Amen!

Today's Focus: *I possess divine supernatural strength to overcome the challenges before me.*

DAY 5:
Preserved For Purpose

Divine, great, and Merciful God; today represents another day that I have been kept, preserved, and blanketed in your love. I rest and take joy in the safety and protection you have provided for my family and me. I am thankful for divine healing; I thank you we are being preserved for Your greater good. I am grateful for each and every waking moment that I have been given to be an expression of divine light, purpose, and power in the earth realm. So be it, and so it is.

Today's Focus: *I am safe, I am divinely protected, and the goodness of God surrounds me.*

DAY 6:
Valuable Relationships

Holy Spirit, provider of all things benevolent and good, I thank you for the blessings you have bestowed upon me this day. I thank you for the kindness and generosity of friends, family, and all of those closest to me. I treasure the relationships that I am privileged to participate in, and I welcome new, healthy relationships that are beneficial to my growth and development. I am thankful for positive assistance, both earthly and divine. I give thanks and praise for all these remarkable and wonderful things! Amen!

Today's Focus: *I am attracting, caring, loving, supportive, healthy relationships.*

DAY 7:
Revive Us Again

Energize me, Holy Spirit, that I may energize the world with enthusiasm and vitality. I pray that even in the darkest of times, social unrest, disease, and famine, there is peace, calm, health, and wholeness worldwide. We are revived and in perfect alignment, even in the midst of what seemingly feels like a loss. Provision and plenty are mine, and any tests that may arise will help me humble myself, overcome and learn the necessary lesson. Amen!

Today's Focus: *Vitality and energy flow through every cell and fiber of my being.*

DAY 8:
The Pain, The Push, The Power

Blessed Spirit of the Most High God, I thank you and give you all the praise for who you are and not only for what you have done. In times of crisis, in times of hurt and pain, you are ever-present and a steadfast hope when things appear to be dismal. Even in what looks dismal, there is an everlasting light. Today we draw on the eternal flame that dwells within and propels us to joy. Today I will sing, laugh, remember yesterday's pain, and recall the pain that pushed me into divine power. This sacred power lives inside me, and I will wield this sacred power to glorify God's Name in all of the earth. Amen!

Today's Focus: *I release the pain and welcome happiness, joy, laughter, and love.*

DAY 9:
Health Is Wealth

Today, I give thanks for divine perfect health, vitality, strength, peace, vibrancy, productivity, fertility and joy. Today I give thanks that my body is operating at its fullest potential and that every cell, muscle, cerebral function, bone, joint, and overall bodily function is in divine order. I am alive; longevity is my inheritance.

Today's Focus: *I honor my body temple; I am well. I am thankful for health and strength.*

DAY 10:
Serenity In The Suffering

Blessings and peace to all who have suffered and are suffering during this season or in this present lifetime; may they find serenity, may dysfunctional patterns of cognition be transformed into divine metacognition. May insight, hope, self-reflection, and self-awareness be made a reality so that healing and wholeness may be a new reality. The things that cause us to be fragmented are now dissolving and becoming whole. We are complete, whole, lacking nothing. I walk in the fullness of joy! My portion is wholeness.

Today's Focus: *I release suffering and pain and embrace total healing wholeheartedly.*

DAY 11:
Expanded Awareness

Gratitude and plentiful thanks I give this day. For this is the day that the Creator has made, and I am rejoicing, and I am glad about it. I give thanks for expansion and that my borders are being enlarged every single day. My mind is expanding, my awareness, my resources are growing, and my vitality is expanding. Today and every day, I walk in dynamic peace and joy. Divine Spirit of the living God, all gratitude, praise, glory, and honor go to you for the beauty you constantly create in our world and beyond. Many thanks. So be it, and so it is, amen.

Today's Focus: *I recognize that gratitude is the precursor to happiness and joy.*

DAY 12:
The Law Of Reciprocity

The sunlight on my face, the warmth and of the rays, the earth, and all its beauty is more than enough to ignite praise from the depths of my soul. Because of the goodness of God and the benefits of walking in faith, we are blessed. The law of reciprocity is real, and I give thanks that what we put out into this world is what we will get back. God, we thank you for universal truths and that in the truth, we are shielded from every negative work and receive the ultimate powerful worker of light, love, joy, peace, and abundance. So be it, and so it is.

Today's Focus: *I choose to shine the inner light of God brightly into all the world.*

DAY 13:
Heal The World

How good it is to be in the space of grace, light, and love. For this space, we are one with the divine presence and power, unified, undifferentiated, and indivisible with the one true and living God. In this prayer field, I give thanks for life, vitality, strength, and divine perfect health. In this awareness, I pray for the health of the planet, recognizing the perfection of all creation, the intricacy and connectedness of all humanity. As a collective body of people, we will prosper at this moment right here and right now. I bless the people, places, and things that I interact with. I bless each area and space that our feet may tread; we are divinely protected, guided, and kept for such a wonderful time as this. It is in this moment that I release and seal this prayer, knowing that it shall not return void but will indeed perform what we have sent it out to do. Amen, and so it is!

Today's Focus: *I embrace my oneness with humanity in the spirit of collective unity.*

DAY 14:
A Brand New Day

I am so very thankful for the opportunity to open my eyes and see a brand-new day; I am grateful for both sunshine and rain. I recognized my oneness with God and am thankful for the unique pre-ordained divine path that I am on that has led me to my highest good and will help me reach my fullest potential. It is in this holy and sacred space that I give thanks. I bless all of those that I have come in contact with; I bless all neighborhoods, countries, towns, nations, and creatures great and small. This prayer is now being released, and I count it done, Amen, ASE, and so it is.

Today's Focus: *I am looking forward to a brand-new day; the past is behind me, and the future is bright.*

DAY 15:
One With God And One With All

For this day and every day, I am thankful; I am grateful for the morning light, and for the sunset. I recognize how interconnected I am with the oneness of God and all of its creation. I am blessed, God is infinite, and abundance is plentiful. In this awareness, I am joyful in the presence and the power of the divine almighty God. There is wholeness, there is divine ageless wisdom, and there is love. I'm thankful, and I bless this planet and your people God. I now release this prayer, knowing that it is done, signed, sealed, and delivered in sacred creativity, and it shall not return to me unfulfilled. So be it, so it is, amen.

Today's Focus: *I am interconnected and interdependent with the oneness of God and all of creation.*

DAY 16:
Living, Moving, In My Being

It is in this precious and divine moment that I recognize that I am walking, talking, living, breathing, seeing, being, and existing as one with the Almighty God who is the one power, one presence, one Creator of all life. I am deeply connected with all that suits my highest good, and that all good things around me are profoundly connected to me. I give thanks for mental clarity, peace, divine perfect love, joy, affection, life, health, and vitality. Those that show up in the world with sickness are now healed. Those who show up in the world with signs of slowing down are now moving in agility, those who show up in the world with fatigue are now rejuvenated, those that were hurting are now happy, where there was pain, peace now reigns and rules, light now floods the space where darkness once resided. This prayer is now released, signed, sealed, and delivered, and what we have put forth in prayer is now ours, so be it, and so it is amen.

Today's Focus: *I am blessed that my body can bend, stretch and flex; I am vibrant and alive!*

DAY 17:
Nothing Missing, Nothing Broken

The power and presence of God is the ultimate divine reality; it is in God that we thrive in strength, love, peace, balance, and wholeness. In God, there is no lack, no failure, no loss. In God, we gain; in God there is only addition; there is only multiplication, no subtraction and no division in God. Abundance, prosperity, wealth, health, light, life, and joy are all in the infinite presence of God. I am at one with this presence that provides and sustains me out of a reservoir that has no end. I am a receptor of God's unlimited supply of goodness, grace, love, peace, and joy. In this divine sacred awareness, I release this prayer in gratitude, with the confidence in knowing that it is done, so be it, and so it is. Amen.

Today's Focus: *I am manifesting and grounding my life in divine right reality in word, thought, and deed.*

DAY 18:
Blessed To Be A Blessing

Today, I am blessed; we are blessed. We are blessed in the city, blessed in the field, blessed in our going out and going in. Our families are blessed, our finances are blessed, our lives are blessed, our health is blessed, our homes are blessed, our resources are blessed with an unlimited supply of blessings that never run out! On this day, we are growing, thriving, and living our best and blessed lives right here and right now! It is with unshakeable faith that we know that it is so, and is already done! Amen and Ase!

Today's Focus: *I am blessed each second, each minute, and every hour of the day.*

DAY 19:
Yes And Amen

The promises of God are yes and amen; I am so thankful that I am not in stagnation because I am an open vessel to manifestation and miracles. I am grateful to give a surrendered yes so that when I make my request known to God, God can then say yes. I am thankful comply with God's mandate on my life, so then, in turn, God w then adhere to the request. And so, at this moment, right here ar right now, gratitude extends from my being, knowing that I am o) with the almighty, boundless, formless, omnipotent power that t human language cannot define. The name of God is holy, and I relea this prayer to a holy God who is complete in of itself. I affirm that t words set forth will not return void, and it is so. Amen.

Today's Focus: *I am confident in the yes, the amen, the so be it, and the so it is that readily flows in my life.*

DAY 20:
Prayer For Immunity

God, you are magnificent, gracious, loving, kind, powerful, and sovereign! I am one with God; I am one with all. On this day and every day, each cell in my body temple is fully operational; every muscle fiber, every neuron, every electron, every synaptic nerve is functioning as it was on the day that I was born. God, I thank you that my blood flows, bone marrow, joints, five senses, the heartbeat, tissues in the body temple are all in divine alignment with the same intention that they were created. I rejoice, knowing that wellness and health are my inheritance. My immune system performs at optimum levels against any foreign body on the planet that has taken up residence in spaces that were not divinely intended. Let there be health, prosperity, and joy in the earth from henceforth, now, and forevermore. I release this prayer, knowing that all is well, and it is so! Amen, so be it!!

Today's Focus: *My immune system is functioning at optimum levels; I am healthy, and I am fearless.*

DAY 21:
We Surrender

On this day and every day, I am so very thankful for my oneness with the one real presence, called LIFE, and my life is the life of God revealing itself daily in the earth. Holy Spirit, I thank you for being the revealing of God in and through all things. Every life form reveals your glory in its fullest expression. The sun, the moon, the stars, the rain, and every creature declares the magnificence of creation. Thanks, praises, and glory belong to no one else, but the Almighty creative force called God. It is God who has made us and not we ourselves; no other power is equal to or worthy to be compared to the glorious power and nature of God that is being revealed in us today and every day. In this sacred prayer field, what has been placed in the atmosphere is now sealed, sent, and on its way to divine action. The word is living, quick, and active. Amen, so be it, and so it is.

Today's Focus: *I am living a productive, dynamic, active, positive, and fruitful life.*

DAY 22:
Gratitude

Lord, you are good, and your mercy endures forever, and gratitude is my portion. I am so very thankful for life, for this is the day that the Lord has made, and I will rejoice and be glad in it. In the stillness and the quiet, I am one with the everlasting presence. I cannot escape this presence, and I can't flee from it, wherever I go, and wherever I rest, that divine abounding presence of peace and love is always there. I am thankful for this day and the opportunity to love, give, embrace, and be. Love is my essence, recognizing that I am connected to the one life, one love, one heartbeat which exists in all and is all. I breathe in peace and exhale joy; I release, reflect, and renew my mind in this prayer field, knowing that the expression of gratitude has been received and heard by The Most High God. It is so, so be it, and so it is. Amen.

Today's Focus: *I am open to receiving goodness and every good gift unmerited and deserved.*

DAY 23:
I Am Free

So thankful am I for this beautiful day, for the light of life, for the peace of the planet, for there will be peace, and I am one with the calm presence, power, and the eternal presence of God who is not confined to shape, space, description or form. God is sovereign, God is Holy, and I am thankful, blessed, happy, strengthened, loved, and comforted by the power of the Almighty God. Healing and deliverance are the children's bread, and as a result of this provision, we are set free and completely healed. I give so much thanks for the ability to stand firm in the countless abundance of God. So be it, and so it is.

Today's Focus: *I am free from all that binds, and I am walking in divine right harmony and liberty.*

DAY 24:
It Is Working For My Good

The power of God is ever sustaining; I am one with this beautiful power and presence that is nameless, formless, boundless, and endless. This presence is non-descriptive as there are not enough adjectives to describe it, it is glorious, and I am one with this miraculous and glorious light. Every cell of my body is being invigorated with its power, love, and light. Each day is a day of divine fulfillment that floods my heart with love and joy. I am thankful for this moment in time; I cherish this day and every day that I am alive on this side of divine reality. So in this moment, I give unrestricted praise and gratitude for everything that is entering my life and everything that is leaving it, knowing that everything cyclical is for my highest good. I release this prayer, I let it go, and I let it be. And so, it is!

Today's Focus: *I am an open conduit to receive an avalanche of abundance and miracles.*

DAY 25:
One Power And One Presence

In this very moment, I am so thankful for the one heartbeat, one li[fe], one power, one presence that is God Almighty. I declare my onene[ss] with the ultimate divine power and presence. This divine presenc[e], called God, is indescribable and amazing. I give thanks every day f[or] the ability to exhale and inhale, to move live, and have my being. I a[m] thankful for the stillness, for the quiet, for the peace, for the ability [to] rest in God. Daily I abide in the grace, peace, and joy of a loving Go[d] who is concerned with every aspect of my life. For this, I am thankf[ul]. In faith, I release the prayer with the realization that it is so! Ame[n] and amen!

Today's Focus: *I guard and protect my heart so that it remains healthy, stress free, and robust.*

DAY 26:
I Speak

I speak life to that which lacks vitality, I speak hope to the hopeless, I speak joy in the midst of sorrow, I speak unity in the midst of division, I speak love in the face of hatred, I speak forgiveness where there are grudges, I speak peace where there is war, I speak revival where there is weariness, I speak oneness with God where we have felt separated, I speak selflessness where there has been selfishness, I speak power where there has been impotence, I speak progress to that which has been stagnant, I speak healing where there has been sickness, and I speak wholeness to that which was broken.

Today's Focus: *I use words that empower, that revive, that rejuvenate, that reinforce and revitalize.*

DAY 27:
Behold The Glory

Holy Spirit, I welcome you each day as I rise to greet the sun. My eyes behold the glory of God manifested in the earth in all of creation. The birds declare your glory and sing your praises; the trees bend their branches at the command of the wind, the rain saturates the earth so that the greenery may grow, providing oxygen to human life balancing out the planetary environment. I am thankful that creation has no choice but to praise and glorify the power and the presence as it was created and designed to do. In this awareness, I give thanks and praises in the Spirit of sweet surrender. With a sincere Ase and amen it is declared to be so.

Today's Focus: *I am filled with the Holy Spirit; the presence of God is operating in us, through us, as us.*

DAY 28:
It's All In Me

Joy unspeakable now floods my soul; peace, life, love, harmony, and victory belong to me today. Every day, safety and security are evident in my life because I am inseparable from the one power, one presence, and one life: God. I am submerged and immersed in this divine love. I recognize the divine ingenuity, intelligence, and creativity of the Creator of all living things, great and small. I take nothing for granted, and I surrender to the sacredness of my life, the purpose of my life, and the calling on my life that drives me into divine destiny. Every day is a day of supreme gratitude and thankfulness for health, energy, and strength. The gratitude extended is not only for what God can do for us but also for the privilege to do the will of the one who has sent us. Here am I, send me! I am available; use me for thy glory! Amen!

Today's Focus: *A river of joy flows into my life with grace and ease and floods my heart with security and serenity.*

DAY 29:
Take Nothing For Granted

Grateful, thankful, and blessed am I to be alive in this very moment in time. The presence and the power of Almighty God are surrounding me, keeping me, guiding me, holding me, and sustaining me. On this great and glorious day, I give thanks unto the Lord, for the mercy of God endures forever, and divine goodness is on constant display. The magnificence and majesty of God cannot be replicated or duplicated. Creation speaks your praises by merely existing. The trees, the leaves, the birds, the bees, the sun, the stars, the moon, and mars all declare your greatness and reflect the life of God. Taking nothing for granted as love and grace daily abound. Amen, Ase, Selah, so be it.

Today's Focus: *I am thankful for all that I have, and I am making space for what has yet to come.*

DAY 30:
Just For You

My prayer for you is that you flourish, grow, expand, and operate fully to reveal the Most High God on the earth. That your light will shine as brightly as the rays of the sun and that your countenance would glow fresh with joyous light. I pray that your health, finances, emotions, and psychological well-being are stabilized now and, in the days to come. I pray that stress would flee, that tension would cease, and that the serenity of the divine "Peace Speaker" would deposit itself fully into your temple with ease, elegance, and grace. May the next chapter of your life grant you the desires of your heart as you delight yourself in the Lord your God, acknowledging your oneness with the power of God; that only operates for your highest good. If we decree a thing, it shall be established, and I declare goodness, safety, protection, favor, grace, love, and peace as your portion all of the days of your life. So it is, and so it shall be, amen.

Today's Focus: *My Focus is on you, the reader, and it is time to go after all that God has for you now and in the future.*

Conclusion

Affirmative prayer is an essential part of my life, and I invite you to use this as a simple guide to begin to formulate your own affirmative prayers. Remember to start your affirmative prayer by recognizing who God is, recognizing your oneness with God and with all of creation. By faith, affirm and speak the positive outcomes even if you do not see them yet. Thank God for the outcome as if it is already done, and then release the prayer in faith, knowing that all is well.

www.ingramcontent.com/pod-product-compliance
Lightning Source LLC
Chambersburg PA
CBHW031439040426
42444CB00006B/885